KEYS FOR THE KIN
Performance Book
Level A

JOSEPH MARTIN DAVID ANGERMAN MARK HAYES

Scripture quoted from THE HOLY BIBLE, NEW INTERNATIONAL VERSION®, NIV®
Copyright © 1973, 1978, 1984, 2011 by Biblica, Inc.®
Used by permission. All rights reserved worldwide.

ISBN 978-1-5400-9069-0

EXCLUSIVELY DISTRIBUTED BY

Visit Hal Leonard Online at
www.halleonard.com

Visit Shawnee Press Online at
www.shawneepress.com

Contact us:
Hal Leonard
7777 West Bluemound Road
Milwaukee, WI 53213
Email: info@halleonard.com

In Europe, contact:
Hal Leonard Europe Limited
42 Wigmore Street
Marylebone, London, W1U 2RN
Email: info@halleonardeurope.com

In Australia, contact:
Hal Leonard Australia Pty. Ltd.
4 Lentara Court
Cheltenham, Victoria, 3192 Australia
Email: info@halleonard.com.au

CONTENTS

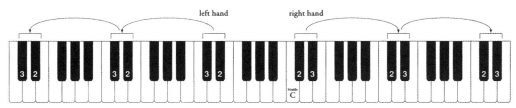

God's Love

Words and Music by Joseph Martin, David Angerman and Mark Hayes

"For great is your love, higher than the heavens . . ." Psalm 108:4a

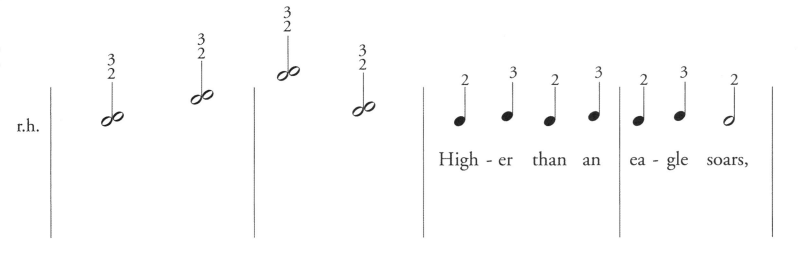

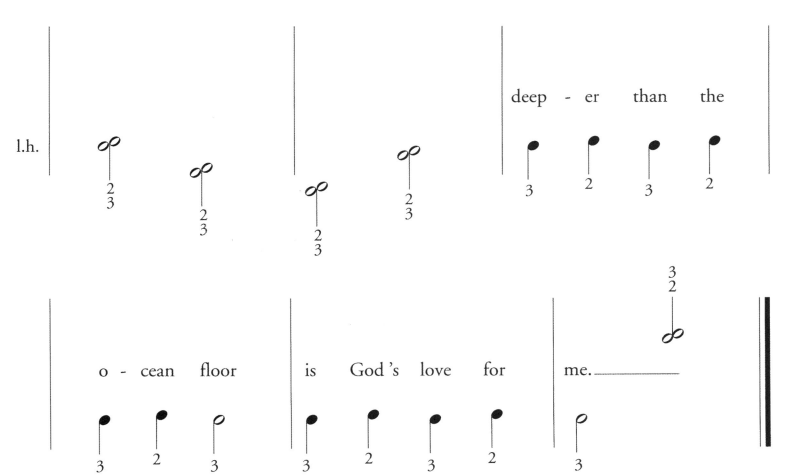

TRAFFIC JAM!

Words and Music by Joseph Martin, David Angerman and Mark Hayes

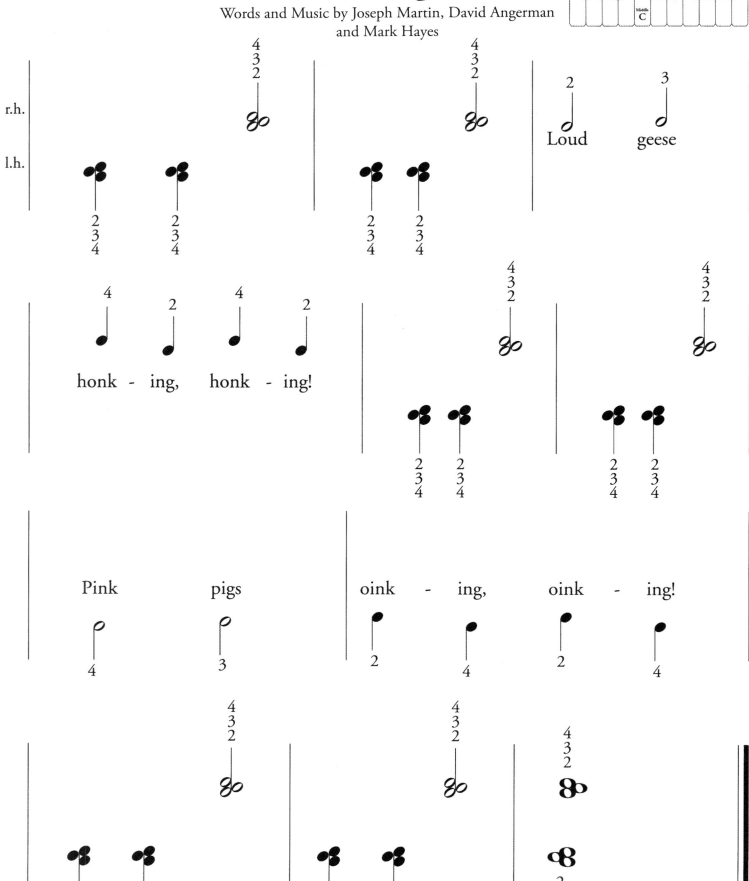

Frog on the Keyboard!

Words and Arrangement by Joseph Martin, David Angerman
and Mark Hayes

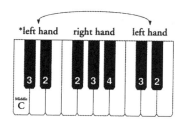

American Folk Melody

r.h.

4   4   4   3   2   4   4   4   4

Frog   on   the   key - board   jump - ing   to   and

l.h.

2   4   4   4   3   2

fro.   Up   on   the   black   notes

2
3

4   4   4   4

leap - ing   high   and

2
o

low.
(hold this note while you
play the rest of the notes
with your left hand)

(l. h. only)*

2
3

2
3

2
3

2
3

2
3

2
3

2
3

*Play these chords with the left hand "jumping" back and forth over the right hand.

I'LL SING ALLELUIA

Arranged by Joseph Martin, David Angerman
and Mark Hayes

*"After this I heard what sounded like the roar
of a great multitude in heaven shouting : Hallelujah!..."* Revelation 19:1

Tune: *Hallelujah*
by William Walker
from *The Sacred Harp*, 1844

r.h.

l.h.

I'll   sing   al - le - lu - ia____ and

you'll   sing   al - le - lu - ia.   We'll

all   sing   al - le - lu - ia____ when

we   ar - rive____ in   heav - en.

 Teacher's part (student part to be played one octave higher)

Flowing

mf

How Firm a Foundation

Arranged by Joseph Martin, David Angerman and Mark Hayes

"See, I lay a stone in Zion, a tested stone, a precious cornerstone for a sure foundation . . ." Isaiah 28:16

Words from
John Rippon's *Selection*, 1787

Tune: *Foundation*
from *The Sacred Harp*, 1844

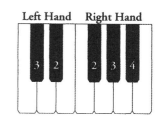

How firm a foun - da - tion, O

saints of the Lord, is _____ laid for your

faith in His ex - cel - lent Word!

 Teacher's part (student part to be played one octave higher)

Moderately

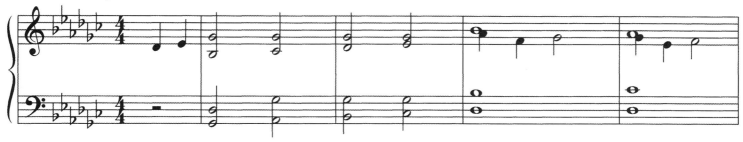

RAINBOW OF PROMISE

 Teacher's part (student part to be played one octave higher than written)

Rainbow of Promise

Words and Music by Joseph Martin, David Angerman and Mark Hayes

"Whenever the rainbow appears in the clouds, I will see it and remember the everlasting covenant . . ." Genesis 9:16a

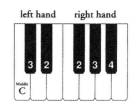

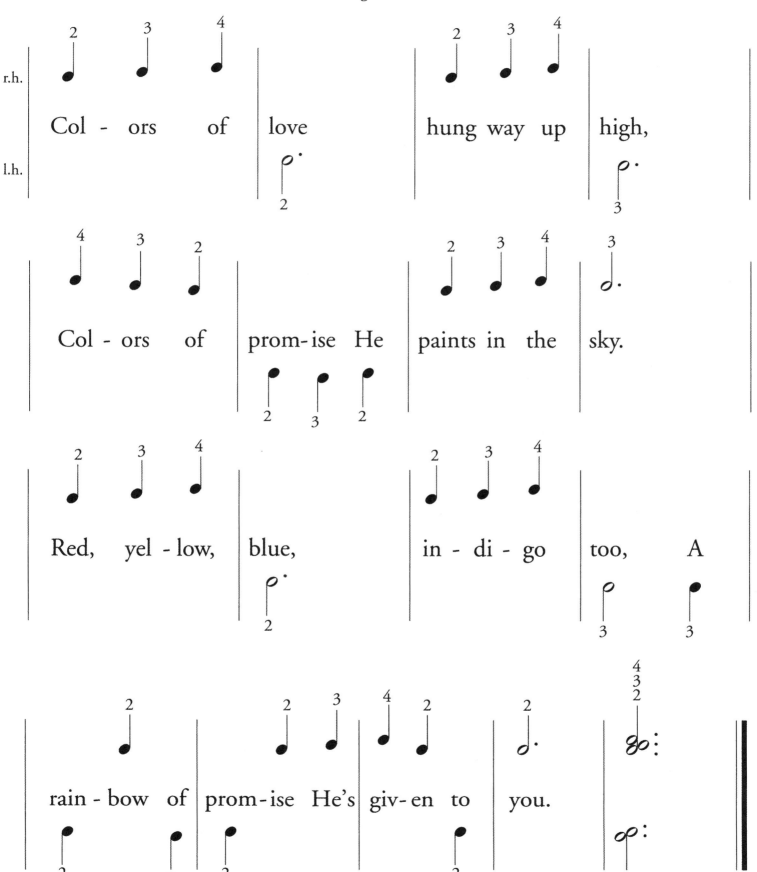

Winter Snow!

Words and Music by Joseph Martin, David Angerman and Mark Hayes

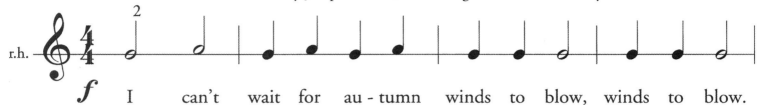

r.h.

f I can't wait for au - tumn winds to blow, winds to blow.

p Soon to fol - low comes the win - ter snow, win - ter snow!

Teacher's part (student part to be played one octave higher than written)

Moderately

f

p

FOLLOW

Words and Music by Joseph Martin, David Angerman
and Mark Hayes

*"Whoever serves me must follow me, and where I am,
my servant also will be . . ."* John 12:26a

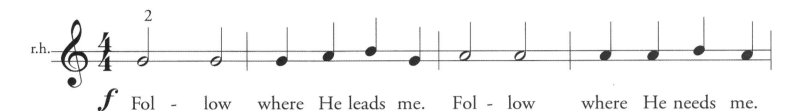

Fol - low where He leads me.   Fol - low   where He needs me.

Fol - low,   please be- lieve me.   I will fol - low Je - sus.

 Teacher's part (student part to be played one octave higher than written)

Lively

SONGS OF FAITH

Words and Music by Joseph Martin, David Angerman and Mark Hayes

"I will sing hymns to your name." Romans 15:9b

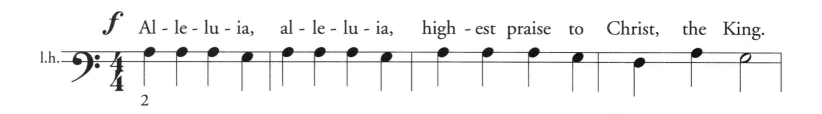

Al - le - lu - ia, al - le - lu - ia, high - est praise to Christ, the King.

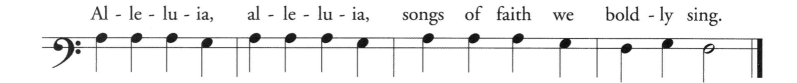

Al - le - lu - ia, al - le - lu - ia, songs of faith we bold - ly sing.

 Teacher's part (student part to be played as written)

Joyfully

CHILDREN OF THE KING

Words and Music by Joseph Martin, David Angerman and Mark Hayes

"Therefore my heart is glad and my tongue rejoices . . ." Psalm 16:9a

f Chil - dren of the King, lift your hearts and sing.

Raise your voice, all re - joice, glad ho - san - nas bring.

 Teacher's part (student part to be played one octave higher than written)

Boldly

'ROUND AND 'ROUND

 Teacher's part (student part to be played as written)

'ROUND AND 'ROUND

Words and Music by Joseph Martin, David Angerman and Mark Hayes

Praise the Lord, all you nations; extol Him all you peoples.
For great is His love toward us . . ."Psalm 117:1-2a

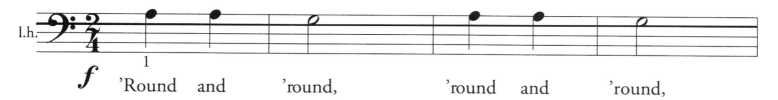

'Round and 'round, 'round and 'round,

All the world His praise re - sounds.

Joy - ful sound! Joy - ful sound!

Ev - 'ry - where His love a - bounds!

GET ON BOARD!

Teacher's part (student part to be played one octave higher than written)

Get On Board!

Arranged by Joseph Martin, David Angerman and Mark Hayes

African-American Spiritual

Get on board, all you chil - dren! Time's a - wast - in'; don't be late! Get on board, all you chil - dren! Head - in' for that Glo - ry day. Run, run! Hur - ry, chil - dren! Run, run! Don't be late! Run, run! Hur - ry, chil - dren! Time's a - wast - in'; don't be late! Time's a - wast - in'; don't be late!

GLORY BE TO GOD

 Teacher's part (student part to be played as written)

GLORY BE TO GOD

Words and Music by Joseph Martin, David Angerman
and Mark Hayes

"Glorify the Lord with me; let us exalt his name together." Psalm 34:3

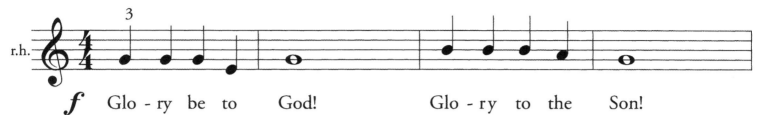

r.h.

f Glo - ry be to God! Glo - ry to the Son!

Glo - ry to the Spir - it! Bless - ed Three in One!

An - gels all re - joice. Now we must add our voice.

Glo - ry be to God and God a - lone! _____

Mary's Little Lamb

Arranged by Joseph Martin, David Angerman and Mark Hayes

"…Look, the Lamb of God, who takes away the sin of the world!" John 1:29b

Traditional

l.h.

p Mar - y had a lit - tle Lamb, lit - tle Lamb, lit - tle Lamb.

Mar - y had a lit - tle Lamb, and Je - sus was His name.

 Teacher's part (student part to be played as written)

Moderately
play both hands 8va throughout

ELIJAH

Arranged by Joseph Martin, David Angerman and Mark Hayes

". . . And Elijah went up to heaven in a whirlwind." II Kings 2:11b

African-American Spiritual

Where, O where is old E - li - jah? Where, O where is

old E - li - jah? Where, O where is old E - li - jah?

Way down in the prom - ised land.

 Teacher's part (student part to be played one octave higher than written)

JESUS, WORK BESIDE ME

Arranged by Joseph Martin, David Angerman and Mark Hayes

"The Lord will guide you always . . ." Isaiah 58:11b

Words by
Allen Eastman Cross (1907)

Tune: *Eudoxia*
by Sabine Baring-Gould (1834-1924)

Je-sus, work be-side me in the dawn of day;

Gent-ly guide Thy ser-vant till the work be done.

Teacher's part (student part to be played one octave higher than written)

Smoothly

KIND SHEPHERD

Arranged by Joseph Martin, David Angerman and Mark Hayes

*He tends his flock like a shepherd: He gathers the lambs in his arms
and carries them close to his heart." Isaiah 40:11a*

Words by
John Swertner (1746-1813), alt.

Die Wanderschaft in dieser Zeit, Herrnhut, c. 1740
from *C. Gregor Choralbuch*, 1784, alt.

p Kind Shep - herd, take each lit - tle lamb in -

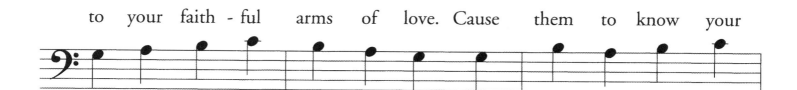

to your faith - ful arms of love. Cause them to know your

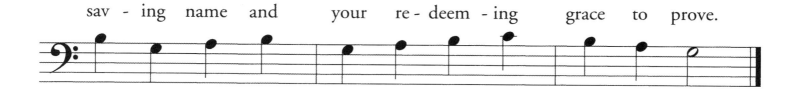

sav - ing name and your re - deem - ing grace to prove.

Teacher's part (student part to be played as written)

Gently

JESUS LOVES ME

 Teacher's part (student part to be played one octave higher than written)

Happily

Jesus Loves Me

Arranged by Joseph Martin, David Angerman and Mark Hayes

"For God so loved the world that he gave His one and only Son . . ." John 3:16a

Words by
Anna B. Warner (1820-1915)

Tune: *Jesus Loves Me*
by William B. Bradbury (1816-1868)

Je-sus loves me! This I know, for the Bi-ble tells me so.

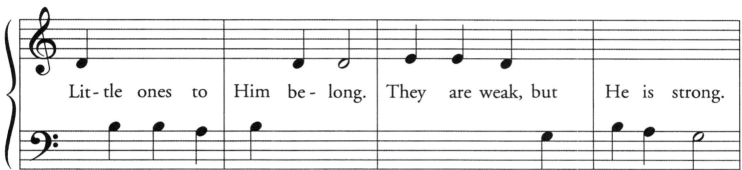

Lit-tle ones to Him be-long. They are weak, but He is strong.

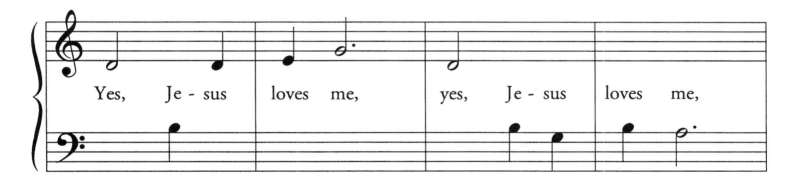

Yes, Je-sus loves me, yes, Je-sus loves me,

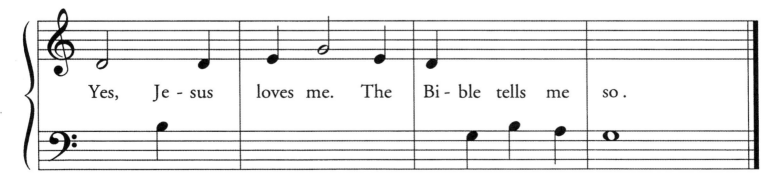

Yes, Je-sus loves me. The Bi-ble tells me so.

I'm a Little Teapot

 Teacher's part (student part to be played one octave higher than written)

Cheerfully

I'm a Little Teapot

Arranged by Joseph Martin, David Angerman and Mark Hayes

American Folk Song

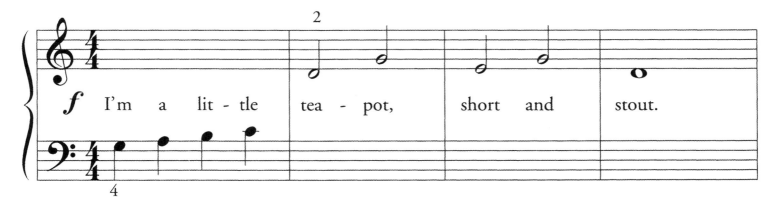

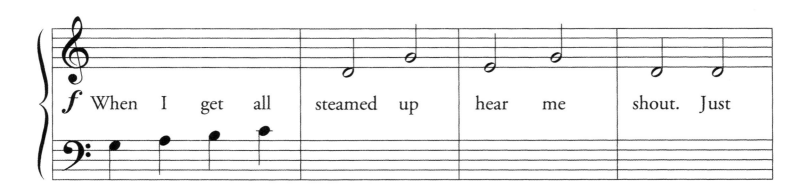

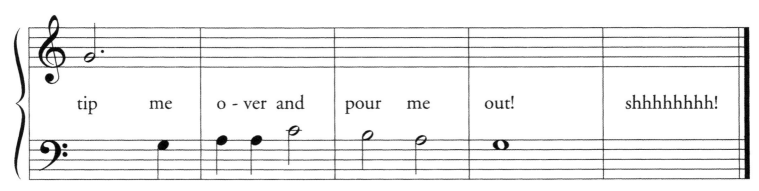

OLD MACDONALD

 Teacher's part (student part to be played one octave higher than written)

Moderately

OLD MacDONALD

Arranged by Joseph Martin, David Angerman and Mark Hayes

American Folk Song

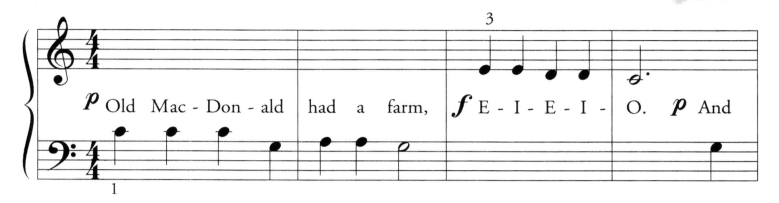

Old Mac - Don - ald had a farm, E - I - E - I - O. And

on this farm he had a duck, E - I - E - I - O!

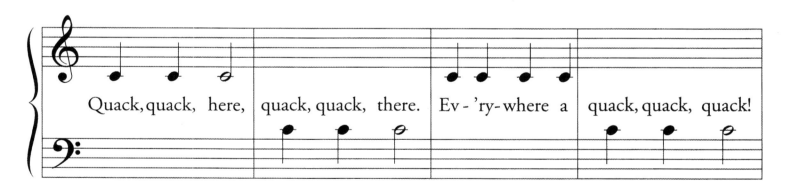

Quack, quack, here, quack, quack, there. Ev - 'ry-where a quack, quack, quack!

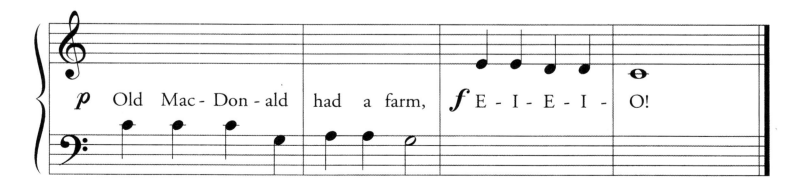

Old Mac - Don - ald had a farm, E - I - E - I - O!

Repeat "Old MacDonald," using different animal names and sounds.

Use with pages 56-60 of Level A

HOLY GOD, WE PRAISE YOUR NAME

 Teacher's part (student part to be played one octave higher than written)

HOLY GOD, WE PRAISE YOUR NAME

Arranged by Joseph Martin, David Angerman and Mark Hayes

"His dominion is an everlasting dominion . . . and his kingdom is one that will never by destroyed." Daniel 7:14b

Paraphrase of *Te Deum* by Ignaz Freuz (1719-1790)
Translated by Clarence Walworth (1820-1900)

Tune: *Grosser gott*
from *Katholisches Gesangbuch*, 1686

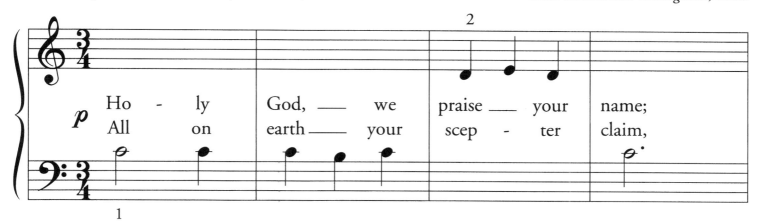

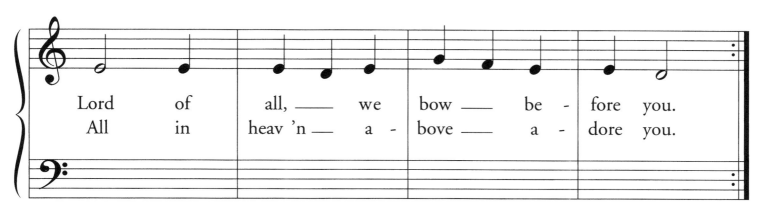

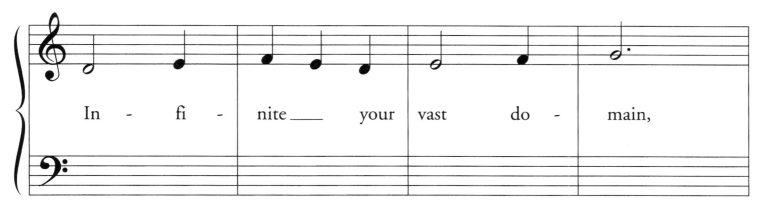

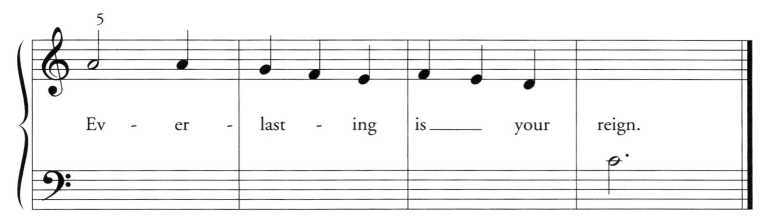